Author's Note

What is it about chocolate that it fascinates one and all? There are hundred adjectives that a chocoholic will use to describe the sweetness of it but for me, chocolate is a journey of discovery! My book *Chocolicious! — Mouth-Watering Vegetarian Chocolate Recipes* is a tribute to all things chocolate that any body can possibly make, create, swoon for in the kitchen. By all means, use this intelligent ingredient in all that you can think of – beverages, cakes, cookies, mousses, moulded titbits, mithais, desserts.

My experiments with chocolate have been work in progress. My experiences with chocolate as an ingredient have been marvelous. So here it is a collection of my superlative experiences that have been put into a good narrative that borders on the sweet!

So start up with a comforting *Warm Chocolate Shots*. Bake *Chocolate Mawa Cupcake or Opera Cake*. Try packs of *Caramel Centered Chocolates* as gifts. And as the grand finale to the book and any of your meals, try the desserts and mithais such as Steamed *Chocolate Pudding* and *Chocolate and Nut Karanji*.

All recipes will serve four (or one or two if there is no reason to share!) and are tried and tested in my kitchen so that you have no difficulty in trying them out

May all chocoholics pass on the good word!

Happy cooking!

Contents

SANJEEV KAPOOR

Chocolicious!

Mouth-Watering Vegetarian Chocolate Recipes

In association with Alyona Kapoor

Popular Prakashan

www.popularprakashan.com

Published by
POPULAR PRAKASHAN PVT. LTD.
301, Mahalaxmi Chambers
22, Bhulabhai Desai Road
Mumbai - 400 026
for Khana Khazana Publications Pvt. Ltd.

First Published 2015

(4421)
ISBN: 978-81-7991-862-3

Design: Anjali Sawant
Photography: Bharat Bhirangi
Food Stylist: Anupa Das

PRINTED IN INDIA
by Saurabh Printers (P) Ltd.
Plot No. 67 A-68, Ecotech, Ext. I
Kasna, Greater Noida-201306 (U.P)

Choco Frappé

INGREDIENTS

6 teaspoons instant coffee powder

8 tablespoons chocolate truffle

4 cups vanilla ice cream

2 cups milk

4 tablespoons powdered sugar

Ice cubes, as required

½ cup whipped cream

Chocolate shavings, for garnishing

METHOD

1. Mix the coffee powder with three teaspoons of warm water to make a decoction.
2. Blend together four tablespoons chocolate truffle, coffee decoction, vanilla ice cream, milk, powdered sugar and ice cubes till smooth. Drizzle the remaining truffle along the sides of four individual glasses to make a pattern. Pour in the coffee-chocolate mixture.
3. Put the whipped cream in a piping bag and pipe over the coffee in each glass. Serve chilled, garnished with chocolate shavings.

Rocky Road Shake

INGREDIENTS

20 marshmallows

4 cups chocolate ice cream

1 cup milk

½ cup roughly chopped walnuts

METHOD

1. Chop the marshmallows.
2. Place half the marshmallows in a blender jar. Add the chocolate ice cream, milk and half the walnuts and blend well.
3. Pour into four individual glasses, garnish with the remaining walnuts and marshmallows.
4. Serve chilled.

Chocolate Lassi

INGREDIENTS

1¼ cups grated dark chocolate

4 cups thick yogurt, chilled

8 tablespoons powdered sugar

A pinch of salt

4 tablespoons dark chocolate chips

METHOD

1. Melt the chocolate in a double boiler. You can also melt the chocolate in a microwave-safe bowl in a microwave on HIGH for thirty seconds. Whisk well and set aside to cool down to room temperature.
2. Mix together the yogurt, sugar and salt in a bowl. Whisk until the sugar and salt are well incorporated.
3. Add the cooled melted chocolate and mix well.
4. Pour into individual glasses and serve chilled, garnished with the chocolate chips.

(Chocolate Lassi)

(Warm Chocolate Shots)

Warm Chocolate Shots

INGREDIENTS

¾ cup chopped dark chocolate

½ cup milk

1 cup chocolate ice cream

2 teaspoons instant coffee powder

2 tablespoons powdered sugar

METHOD

1. Place the dark chocolate in a deep microwave-safe bowl and melt in the microwave on HIGH for thirty seconds. Alternatively, melt the chocolate in a double boiler. Remove and whisk well.
2. Heat the milk in a non-stick pan, but do not boil it. Add it to the chocolate and mix well. Add the chocolate ice cream and mix well.
3. Mix the instant coffee powder in two tablespoons of warm water and add this to chocolate-milk mixture. Add the powdered sugar and mix well.
4. Pour the mixture into eight shot glasses and serve warm.

Mango Milkshake with Chocolate

INGREDIENTS

2 cups fresh mango pulp

4 tablespoons chocolate sauce

4 cups milk

4 tablespoons milk powder

8 tablespoons sugar

2 cups vanilla ice cream

4 tablespoons chocolate chips

METHOD

1. Drizzle chocolate sauce along the sides of four individual glasses and refrigerate for fifteen to twenty minutes.
2. Blend mango pulp, milk, milk powder, sugar and vanilla ice cream till smooth. (If you are using tinned mango pulp, use only four tablespoons of sugar.)
3. Pour into the prepared glasses and serve chilled, garnished with the chocolate chips.

Spiced Hot Chocolate

INGREDIENTS

2 star anise

4 one-inch cinnamon sticks

1 cup chopped dark chocolates

4 cups milk

2 cups fresh cream

¼ cup caster sugar

METHOD

1. Heat the milk, cream and caster sugar together in a non-stick pan but do not let it boil.
2. Remove from the heat and transfer the hot mixture into a bowl. Add the star anise and cinnamon, cover with cling film and set aside for two to three hours.
3. Strain the mixture into another non-stick pan and heat it again.
4. Put chopped chocolate into four individual glasses and pour the hot spiced milk into each glass. Stir well till the chocolate melts.
5. Serve hot.

Nutella Toast

INGREDIENTS

8 tablespoons Nutella

16 slices brown bread

24 walnut kernels, roasted and chopped

METHOD

1. Cut the bread into round slices with a round cookie cutter.
2. Heat a non-stick tawa and toast the bread, from both sides, till crisp.
3. Apply Nutella evenly on all the bread slices. Sprinkle the chopped walnuts on eight slices, cover them with the remaining eight slices.
4. Serve.

Chocolate Baked Yogurt

INGREDIENTS

¼ cup melted dark chocolate

2 tablespoons dark chocolate chips

125 grams yogurt

100 grams condensed milk

100 grams fresh cream

Chocolate powder, for dusting

METHOD

1. Preheat the oven to 180°C/350°F/Gas Mark 4.
2. Pour the yogurt, condensed milk and fresh cream into a bowl and mix well together.
3. Put one-fourth of the yogurt mixture into a glass bowl, add the melted chocolate and mix well. Add this mixture and chocolate chips to the remaining yogurt mixture and mix well. Pour the chocolate-yogurt mixture into four individual oven-proof glasses.
4. Place them in the preheated oven and bake for eight to ten minutes. Remove from the oven and let them cool down to room temperature. Chill in the refrigerator, dust with chocolate powder and serve.

Chocolate Danish

INGREDIENTS

8 tablespoons chopped dark chocolate

2¾ cups refined flour + ¼ cup for layering + for dusting

1½ teaspoons salt

2 tablespoons milk powder

2 tablespoons fresh yeast

1 tablespoon sugar

1¼ cups butter

Milk, as required

METHOD

1. Sift together the flour, salt and milk powder into a bowl. Dissolve the yeast and sugar in two tablespoons lukewarm water in another small bowl.
2. Add the yeast mixture and one-fourth cup butter to the flour mixture. Add sufficient water and knead into a medium-hard dough. Flatten the dough slightly, wrap in cling film and chill for an hour in the refrigerator. To make the butter layering, cream one cup butter till smooth. Add one-fourth cup flour and mix well.
3. Dust a silicon sheet with some flour or line an eight-inch rectangular tray with butter paper. Place the butter mixture on it and shape it into a rectangle. Refrigerate for an

hour or till it is almost hard. Remove the dough from the refrigerator and roll it into a rectangle at least three times the size of the butter rectangle.

4. Place the butter rectangle in the centre of the rolled out dough, fold over the two smaller sides first and then fold over the two longer sides and seal well to enclose the butter entirely. Ensure that the butter is not too hard while placing it on the dough. Wrap in cling film and keep it in the refrigerator for fifteen to twenty minutes.
5. Remove from the refrigerator and roll out into a half-inch thick, seven-inch by five-inch rectangle. Give it a threefold - first fold one-third of the longer side of the rectangle, then fold over the rest to overlap the first fold to make a rectangle again. Wrap in cling film and refrigerate again for half an hour. Remove from the refrigerator and repeat the above process. Wrap in cling film. Refrigerate again for half an hour.
6. Remove from the refrigerator and roll out into half inch thickness. Cut into three-inch squares. Place a little chopped chocolate in the centre of each square, apply a little water on the edges and join the diagonally opposite corners to make a triangle.
7. Arrange the prepared Chocolate Danish on a greased baking tray, cover with a damp piece of muslin and allow them to prove for twenty to twenty-five minutes.
8. Preheat the oven to 180°C/350°F/Gas Mark 4.
9. Uncover the tray and apply a milk wash on the triangles. Bake in the preheated oven for twenty minutes or till light golden in colour. Serve hot.

Chocolate Rum Balls

INGREDIENTS

2 cups crumbled chocolate sponge cake

2 tablespoons rum

½ cup crushed walnut kernels

½ cup crushed almonds

½ cup chocolate sauce

Coating

50 grams chopped dark chocolate

1 tablespoon cream

METHOD

1. Mix together the crumbled cake, walnuts, almonds, chocolate sauce and rum to make a soft dough. Divide into ten equal portions and shape them into balls. Place them in the refrigerator.
2. To make the coating, melt the chocolate in a double boiler. Add the cream and mix well. Set aside to cool.
3. Coat the rum balls with this mixture and chill them again before serving.

(Chocolate Rum Balls)

(Chocolate Mawa Cupcake)

Chocolate Mawa Cupcake

INGREDIENTS

½ cup chocolate chips

200 grams mawa/khoya, crumbled

140 grams refined flour

½ teaspoon baking powder

½ teaspoon soda bicarbonate

120 grams butter

250 grams (1 cup) condensed milk

1 teaspoon vanilla essence

80 ml milk

METHOD

1. Preheat the oven to 180°C/350°F/Gas Mark 4.
2. Sift the flour with baking powder and soda bicarbonate into a deep bowl.
3. In another bowl, cream the butter and condensed milk together till light and fluffy. Add the vanilla essence and mix well.

4. Fold the flour lightly into the butter mixture. Add the milk and mawa and mix well.
5. Arrange the cupcake moulds on a baking tray and pour the batter evenly into each mould. Do not fill them up to the top.
6. Sprinkle chocolate chips on top and place the tray in the preheated oven. Bake for twenty to twenty-five minutes.
7. Remove from moulds and serve.

Eggless Brownie

INGREDIENTS

100 grams dark chocolate, grated

1⅓ cups refined flour

2 teaspoons baking powder

130 grams butter

1 cup + 1½ tablespoons caster sugar

1 teaspoon vanilla essence

½ cup chopped walnuts

½ cup milk

METHOD

1. Preheat oven to 180°C/350°F/Gas Mark 4. Grease an eight-inch square cake tin.
2. Sift the flour and baking powder together into a bowl. Combine together the chocolate and butter in a large microwave bowl and soften, uncovered, for a minute in the microwave oven on HIGH. Alternatively, melt it in a double boiler.
4. Beat in the caster sugar and vanilla essence and blend well. Add the flour mixture, chopped walnuts and milk and mix well.

5. Pour the mixture into the greased cake tin.
6. Bake in the preheated oven for twenty-five to thirty minutes. Remove from the oven and transfer to a wire rack to cool. Cut into squares and serve.

Note: A double boiler is easily installed. Take a small vessel and pour some water in it. Allow it to come to a boil. Place the ingredients that need to be cooked or melted in another vessel that is larger in size. Place the larger vessel on the smaller one and allow the steam from the boiling water to cook/melt the ingredients.

Opera Cake

INGREDIENTS

210 grams refined flour

¾ teaspoon baking powder

¾ teaspoon soda bicarbonate

180 grams butter

300 grams condensed milk

1 teaspoon vanilla essence

112 ml milk

Butter Cream

1½ cups chopped dark chocolate

500 grams butter

500 grams icing sugar

2 tablespoons coffee powder

4 tablespoons Nutella

¾ cup fresh cream

Sugar Syrup

1 cup sugar

METHOD

1. Preheat the oven to 180°C/350°F/Gas Mark 4. Grease a five-and-a-half-inch round cake tin.
2. Sift the flour, baking powder and soda bicarbonate together into a bowl. Cream the butter and condensed milk together in another bowl till fluffy. Add the vanilla essence and mix well. Fold in the flour into the butter mixture gently, adding the milk as you mix. Transfer the batter into the greased cake tin and bake for twenty to twenty-five minutes. Remove the cake from the oven and leave the cake in the tin for five minutes to cool slightly. Turn out onto a wire rack, and leave to cool.
3. To make the butter cream, cream the butter and icing sugar together in a bowl till light and fluffy. Divide the mixture into three equal parts to make three different flavoured butter creams. To make coffee-butter cream, heat one-fourth cup water and add

coffee powder and mix well. Take one portion of the butter cream and add the coffee decoction to it. Mix well and set aside.

4. To make the hazelnut-butter cream, take the second portion of the butter cream and add Nutella to it. Mix well and set aside.
5. To make the chocolate-butter cream, heat the fresh cream in a non-stick pan. Add the chopped chocolate to it and mix well till the chocolate melts. Divide this mixture into two and add the third portion of the butter cream to one portion of the choco-cream mixture.
6. To make sugar syrup, boil one cup water in a deep non-stick pan. Add sugar to it and stir till it dissolves completely. Remove from heat and set aside. Cut the cake horizontally into seven equal layers.
7. Place one layer on a worktop and drizzle with some sugar syrup. Spread half the coffee-butter cream evenly on it. Place the second layer on top of the first layer and drizzle with some sugar syrup. Spread half the hazelnut-butter cream evenly on it. Place the third layer on top of the second layer and drizzle with some sugar syrup. Spread half the chocolate-butter cream evenly on it.
8. Repeat the above procedure for the fourth, fifth and sixth layers. Place the seventh layer on the top and keep in the refrigerator for an hour. Remove the layered cake from the refrigerator and trim the edges to give it a good finish. Pour the remaining choco-cream mixture on top and decorate as you wish. Cut into wedges or pieces and serve.

Eggless Black Forest Gâteau

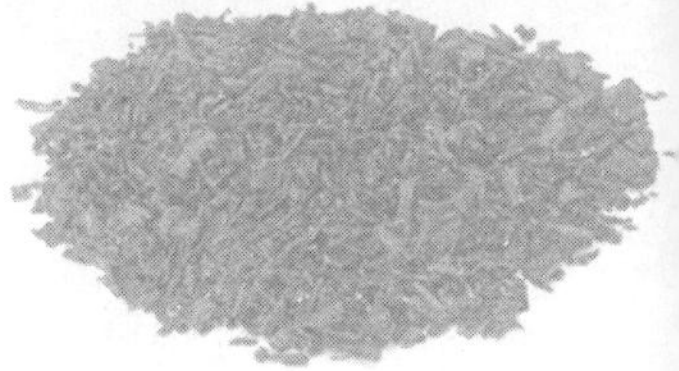

INGREDIENTS

50 grams cocoa powder

Chocolate curls or grated chocolate, as required

110 grams refined flour

½ teaspoon baking powder

½ teaspoon soda bi-carbonate

120 grams butter

200 grams condensed milk

1 teaspoon vanilla essence

5 tablespoons milk

½ cup tinned cherries, with syrup

2 cups whipping cream

METHOD

1. Preheat the oven to 180°C/350°F/Gas Mark 4. Grease a five-and-a-half-inch round cake tin.
2. Sift the flour, cocoa powder, baking powder and soda bicarbonate together into a bowl.

3. Cream the butter and condensed milk together in another bowl till fluffy. Add the vanilla essence and mix well.
4. Fold the flour into the butter mixture gently, adding the milk as you mix. Transfer the mixture into the greased cake tin and bake for twenty to twenty-five minutes.
5. Remove the cake from the oven and leave the cake in the tin for five minutes to cool slightly. Turn out onto a wire rack, and leave to cool.
6. Cut the cake into half horizontally and sprinkle each half with cherry syrup from the tinned cherries.
7. Whip the cream until stiff. Place the bottom half of the cake on a serving plate and spread half the whipped cream over it. Cover with the top half of the cake. Spread the remaining cream over the top and sides.
8. Decorate the gâteau with chocolate curls or grated chocolate and cherries and chill in the refrigerator.
9. Cut into wedges and serve chilled.

Pressure-Cooked Eggless Chocolate Cake

INGREDIENTS

100 grams dark cooking chocolate

1 cup butter

1⅓ cups refined flour

2 teaspoons baking powder

1 cup + 2 tablespoons powdered sugar

1 teaspoon vanilla essence

¾ cup milk

½ cup walnuts kernels

Butter, for greasing

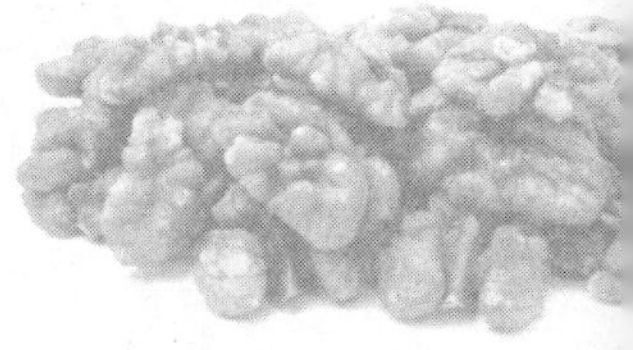

METHOD

1. Add two cups water in a pressure cooker. Place a stainless steel stand in such a way that the cake tin does not come in direct contact with the water.

2. Grate the chocolate. Set aside. Cut the butter into cubes. Melt butter and chocolate in a microwave-safe bowl in the microwave oven on HIGH for one minute.

3. In another bowl sift flour and baking powder.

4. Mix the melted butter and chocolate well. Add powdered sugar, vanilla essence and mix. Add the flour mixture and mix. Correct the consistency by adding milk. Add walnuts and mix gently.
5. Transfer the mixture into a small non-stick square cake tin. Place the cake tin on the stainless steel stand kept inside the cooker. Put the lid on the cooker but without the weight and place it on heat and cook for seventy-five to ninety minutes or till done.
6. To check whether it is done or not, insert a skewer in the cake and if it comes out clean, the cake is done. Remove tin from cooker and let it stand for five minutes.
7. Remove cake from the tin and cool on a wire rack. Slice into wedges and serve.

Chocolate Rocks

INGREDIENTS

250 grams dark chocolate, grated

½ cup almonds, chopped

¼ cup cashew nuts, chopped

¼ cup pistachios, chopped

¼ cup raisins

METHOD

1. Dry-roast the almonds, cashew nuts and pistachios in a non-stick pan on low heat till lightly browned. Remove from the heat and add the raisins and mix well.
2. Melt the chocolate in a double boiler. Whisk till smooth. Add the roasted dried fruit to the melted chocolate in batches. Mix well.
3. Place a spoonful of the choco-nut mixture on a silicon sheet and shape into a ball. You can also use a butter paper instead of silicon sheet. Roll the rest of the chocolate mixture in the same way.

4. Place the silicon sheet on a tray and keep it in the refrigerator for fifteen to twenty minutes.
5. Serve immediately. You can wrap the balls up and use the candy as gifts.

Chocolate Shells

INGREDIENTS

1 cup chopped dark chocolate

METHOD

1. Wipe the chocolate moulds clean and dry with tissue paper. Melt the chocolate in a double boiler. Remove from heat and stir well to temper the chocolate till the temperature falls to 30°C.
2. Pour the melted chocolate into the moulds, covering the sides evenly.
3. Turn the moulds upside down over a bowl and scrape off the dripping excess chocolate. Rest the moulds on a cooling rack till set. Use as required.

Pralines

INGREDIENTS

2 cups chopped dark chocolate

Nougat

½ cup sugar

½ cup chopped nuts
(cashew nuts, almonds)

METHOD

1. To make nougat, caramelise the sugar in a non-stick pan till light brown. Add the chopped nuts and mix well till the caramel coats them evenly.
2. Remove the mixture from the heat and spread evenly on a silicon mat. Allow it to cool. When cooled, crush it lightly.
3. Wipe the chocolate moulds clean and dry with a tissue paper.

4. Melt the chocolate in a double boiler. Remove from heat and stir well to temper the chocolate till the temperature falls to 32°C.
5. Pour a little melted chocolate into the moulds, covering the sides evenly.
6. Holding the moulds upside down over a bowl, scrape off dripping excess chocolate. Rest upright on a cooling rack till set.
7. Place one teaspoon of crushed nougat into each shell.
8. Melt the remaining chocolate again in a microwave and stir till the temperature falls to 32°C. Pour the melted chocolate on top of the nougat and spread it evenly with a scraper. Scrape off the excess chocolate. Rest upright on a cooling rack till set.
9. Remove from moulds and serve.

Chocolate Paan

INGREDIENTS

1 cup chopped milk chocolate

2 ready-made meetha paan

METHOD

1. Wipe the chocolate moulds clean and dry with a tissue paper..
2. Place the chocolate in a microwave-safe bowl and melt in a microwave on HIGH for one minute. Remove the bowl from the microwave and whisk well till the temperature comes down to 30°C.
3. Pour the melted chocolate in the moulds and rotate them so that the sides of the moulds are coated evenly.
4. Turn the moulds upside down over the bowl to drip off the excess chocolate. Rest the moulds on a cooling rack till set.

5. Coarsely blend the paan in the blender. Divide the paan mixture into as many equal portions as the number of moulds and stuff the mixture into the prepared chocolate shells.
6. Melt the remaining chocolate again in the microwave on HIGH for one minute. Remove from the microwave and whisk well till the temperature comes down to 30 °C.
7. Pour the melted chocolate on top of the paan stuffing. Scrape off any excess chocolate.
8. Refrigerate the moulds for ten to fifteen minutes or till the chocolate sets.
9. Remove from moulds and serve.

(Chocolate Paan)

(Crispy Puffed Rice Bar)

Crispy Puffed Rice Bar

INGREDIENTS

2 cups puffed rice

2 tablespoons butter + for greasing

½ cup grated dark chocolate

1 tablespoon peanut butter

½ cup roasted and crushed peanuts

½ cup grated white chocolate

METHOD

1. Heat one tablespoon butter in a non-stick pan. Add the dark chocolate and once it melts, add one cup puffed rice, half tablespoon peanut butter and half the crushed peanuts. Mix well. Grease a five-inch by seven-inch aluminum tray with butter. Spread the mixture evenly into the tray and set aside.
2. Repeat the above procedure with white chocolate and remaining ingredients. Spread this evenly on top of the dark chocolate layer.
3. Allow to cool to room temperature and refrigerate for fifteen to twenty minutes. Cut into desired shapes and serve.

Moulded Chocolate

INGREDIENTS

1 cup chopped dark chocolate

1 cup chopped milk chocolate

Filling

1 cup fresh cream

2 teaspoons caster sugar

1 tablespoon strawberry crush

¾ tablespoon instant coffee powder

METHOD

1. Wipe the chocolate moulds clean and dry with a tissue paper.
2. To make dark chocolate shells, melt the dark chocolate in a double boiler. Remove from the heat and stir well to temper the chocolate till the temperature falls to 32°C.
3. Pour the melted chocolate into the moulds, covering the sides evenly. Turn the moulds upside down over a bowl and scrape the dripping excess chocolate. Rest on a cooling rack till set.

4. To make milk chocolate shells, melt the milk chocolate in a double boiler. Remove from heat and stir well to temper the chocolate till the temperature falls to 30°C.
5. Pour the melted chocolate into the moulds, covering the sides evenly. Turn the moulds upside down over a bowl and scrape the dripping excess chocolate. Rest on a cooling rack till set.
6. To make the filling, heat the cream in a non-stick pan. Add the caster sugar and stir till the sugar melts. Take the pan off the heat and divide the mixture equally into two bowls.
7. Add the strawberry crush to one bowl and coffee powder to the other. Mix well.
8. Pour the strawberry filling into the dark chocolate shells. Do not fill them completely.
9. Melt the remaining dark chocolate again in a microwave. Remove from the oven and stir well to temper the chocolate till the temperature falls to 32°C.
10. Pour the melted chocolate over the filled shells and with the help of a scraper spread a thin layer on top of the mould and scrape off the excess chocolate.
11. Refrigerate the moulds for ten to fifteen minutes or till the chocolate sets.

12. Pour the coffee filling into the milk chocolate shells. Do not fill them completely.
13. Melt the remaining milk chocolate again in a microwave. Remove from the oven and stir well to temper the chocolate till the temperature falls to 30°C.
14. Pour the melted chocolate on top of the filled shells and with the help of a scraper spread a thin layer on top of the mould and scrape off the excess chocolate.
15. Refrigerate the moulds for ten to fifteen minutes or till the chocolate sets.
16. Remove from mould and serve

Caramel Centered Chocolates

INGREDIENTS

1 cup chopped milk chocolate

1 cup condensed milk

METHOD

1. Wipe the chocolate moulds clean and dry with a tissue paper.
2. Melt the chocolate in a double boiler. Remove from the heat and stir it well to temper the chocolate till the temperature falls to 30°C.
3. Pour the melted chocolate into the moulds, covering the sides evenly.
4. Turn the moulds upside down over a bowl and scrape off the excess dripping chocolate. Rest on a cooling rack till set.
5. Heat the condensed milk in a non-stick pan. Cook till the mixture turns light brown in colour. As it starts thickening, take the pan off the heat and set aside to cool.

6. Pour the cooked condensed milk into piping bags and pipe into the prepared chocolate shells. Do not fill them completely.
7. Melt the remaining chocolate again in a microwave. Remove from the oven and stir well to temper the chocolate till the temperature falls to 30°C.
8. Pour the melted chocolate on top of the filled shells and with the help of a scraper spread a thin layer on top of the mould and scrape off the excess chocolate.
9. Refrigerate the moulds for ten to fifteen minutes or till the chocolate sets. Remove from moulds and serve.

Wafer Chocolate

INGREDIENTS

1 cup chopped dark chocolate

¼ cup chopped white chocolate

8 wafer biscuits

1 cup condensed milk

4 tablespoons crushed butterscotch pearls

METHOD

1. Cook the condensed milk in a non-stick pan on low heat, stirring continuously, till it develops a toffee-like texture and is reduced to half its original volume. Take the pan off the heat and set aside.
2. Arrange four wafer biscuits on a large plate and apply the reduced condensed milk on one side of each wafer biscuit.
3. Sprinkle one tablespoon crushed butterscotch pearls on each of these four wafer biscuits. Drizzle a little of the reduced condensed milk. Cover with the remaining four wafer biscuits to make sandwiches. Press very lightly.

4. Melt the dark chocolate in a microwave-safe bowl in a microwave oven on HIGH for one minute and let it cool.
5. Dip the wafer biscuit sandwiches in the melted dark chocolate and coat them evenly, turning them with a fork. Place on a wire rack.
6. Tap the sandwiches lightly so that the excess chocolate drips down. Refrigerate for ten to fifteen minutes or till set.
7. Melt the white chocolate in a microwave-safe bowl in a microwave oven on HIGH for thirty seconds. Cool and pour into a small piping bag with pointed nozzle. Drizzle over the prepared chocolates in a pattern.
8. Serve when set.

(Wafer Chocolate)

(Chocolate and Cheese Sandwich)

Chocolate and Cheese Sandwich

INGREDIENTS

2 cups grated dark chocolate

1 cup grated processed cheese + for garnishing

12 white bread slices

4 tablespoons butter

2 tablespoons chocolate shavings

METHOD

1. Preheat a sandwich grill.
2. Butter all the bread slices on one side. Divide the grated chocolate and grated cheese into eight portions each.
3. Place four slices of bread, buttered side up, on a worktop. Spread one portion each of the chocolate and cheese on the four slices. Cover with four more bread slices, keeping the buttered side up.

4. Spread one portion each of the chocolate and cheese on the bread slices. Cover with the remaining slices, keeping the buttered side up.
5. Place in the sandwich grill, but do not close the lid. Grill till the bottom side is golden and then turn over the sandwich and grill the other side similarly.
6. Remove from grill, place on a serving platter. Sprinkle with chocolate shavings and grated cheese. Serve immediately.

Chocolate Coated Nuts

INGREDIENTS

½ cup chopped dark chocolate

¼ cup chopped white chocolate

12 almonds

12 cashew nuts

METHOD

1. Roast the almonds and cashew nuts in a non-stick pan till light brown. Take the pan off the heat and spread the roasted nuts on a tray to cool.
2. Place the dark chocolate in a microwave-safe bowl and melt in a microwave oven on HIGH for thirty seconds. Take the pan off the heat and allow the chocolate to cool, stirring continuously, to 30°C.
3. Dip the roasted nuts in the melted chocolate. Using a fork, place the nuts on a silicon sheet or butter paper. Refrigerate for fifteen to twenty minutes.

4. Place the white chocolate in a microwave-safe bowl and melt in a microwave oven on HIGH for thirty seconds. Take the pan off the heat and allow the chocolate to cool, stirring continuously, to 30^{0}C.

5. Pour the melted white chocolate in a piping bag with a pointed nozzle and drizzle an attractive design on the coated nuts. Refrigerate for ten minutes.

6. Serve chilled.

Chocoholic

INGREDIENTS

¾ cup melted milk chocolate

¾ cup melted white chocolate

¾ cup melted dark chocolate

1½ cups fresh cream

1½ cups whipped cream

4 teaspoons chocolate powder, or
4 teaspoons white chocolate chips

METHOD

1. Heat the fresh cream in a non-stick pan. When it is about to come to a boil, remove the pan from heat.
2. In a glass bowl, add the milk chocolate and half cup of hot fresh cream. Whisk well and set aside to cool. Once cooled, fold in half cup of whipped cream and mix well. Set aside.

3. Repeat this same procedure using the melted white chocolate and melted dark chocolate as well.
4. Pour the three types of prepared mousse into three different piping bags.
5. Take four individual shot glasses and fill one-third of each glass with the milk chocolate mousse. Refrigerate for fifteen minutes or till set.
6. Remove from the refrigerator and top it up with the white chocolate mousse so that each shot glass is about two-third full. Refrigerate for fifteen minutes or till set.
7. Remove from the refrigerator and fill up all the shot glasses with dark chocolate mousse. Sprinkle each with chocolate powder.
8. Refrigerate for half an hour at least and serve chilled.

{**Note:** You can serve this decorated with white chocolate chips.}

Chocolate Coated Fresh Fruit

INGREDIENTS

½ medium apple, cut into ½-inch cubes

¼ medium pineapple, cut into ½-inch cubes

2 elaichi bananas, cut into ½-inch thick round slices

½ medium pear, cut into ½-inch cubes

2 cups chopped dark chocolate

¼ cup chopped white chocolate

METHOD

1. Melt the dark chocolate in a microwave-safe bowl on microwave HIGH for one minute. Allow it to cool to room temperature, stirring continuously.
2. Pierce toothpicks in the fruit pieces and dip into the melted chocolate.
3. Place the chocolate dipped fruit on butter paper or a silicon sheet. Refrigerate for thirty minutes.

4. Melt the white chocolate in a microwave-safe bowl on microwave HIGH for one minute. Allow it to cool down to room temperature.
5. Pour the melted white chocolate into a piping bag with a thin nozzle and pipe over the fruit pieces, making a zigzag pattern. Refrigerate for ten minutes or more. Serve chilled.

Chocolate Sauce

INGREDIENTS

4 tablespoons cocoa powder

2 cups milk

½ cup sugar

¼ cup frozen butter, cut into ½-inch pieces

METHOD

1. Mix the milk and cocoa powder together in a non-stick pan. Bring it to a boil and simmer, stirring continuously, till it thickens.
2. Add the sugar and continue to cook, stirring continuously. Add the chopped butter and mix well. Serve warm.

(Chocolate Coated Fresh Fruit)

(Steamed Chocolate Pudding)

Steamed Chocolate Pudding

INGREDIENTS

1¼ cups chopped white chocolate

½ cup milk

2 tablespoons butter

½ cup condensed milk

½ teaspoon vanilla essence

1 cup fresh white breadcrumbs

¼ cup chopped walnuts

METHOD

1. Boil the milk in a deep non-stick pan. Place the chocolate in a bowl, add the boiling milk and mix well.
2. Put the butter in another bowl, add the condensed milk and vanilla essence and blend till creamy. Add the milk-chocolate mixture and mix well. Add the breadcrumbs and walnuts and mix well. Boil sufficient water in a steamer.
3. Pour the prepared batter into silicon cupcake moulds and place in the steamer. Steam on medium heat for thirty minutes. Remove from mould and serve warm.

Chocolate Kulfi

INGREDIENTS

½ cup grated dark chocolate
1 litre (5 cups) full-cream buffalo milk
5 green cardamoms, crushed
1 tablespoon crushed cashew nuts
1 tablespoon crushed pistachios
1 tablespoon crushed almonds
½ cup condensed milk
1 tablespoon cashew nut paste

METHOD

1. Bring the milk to a boil in a deep non-stick pan.
2. Add the crushed green cardamoms and simmer, stirring, for twenty-five to thirty minutes, or till it is reduced to half its original volume.
3. Add the crushed cashew nuts, pistachios and almonds and mix well and continue to simmer.

4. Remove the cardamom skins and continue to simmer for twenty minutes or till the milk is reduced to one-third its original volume.
5. Add the condensed milk and cashew nut paste and mix well. Add the grated chocolate and take the pan off the heat and set aside to cool.
6. Pour into kulfi moulds and keep in the freezer to set for six to eight hours.
7. Unmould and serve.

Chocolate Ice Cream

INGREDIENTS

¾ cup chopped dark chocolate

½ cup dark chocolate chips

1 cup milk

1 cup milk powder

1¼ cups + 2 tablespoons fresh cream

½ cup powdered sugar

METHOD

1. Heat one-fourth cup milk in a small non-stick pan and add milk powder to it. Mix well till well blended, ensuring that there are no lumps.
2. Take the pan off the heat and set aside to cool. Place the remaining three-fourth cup milk in the refrigerator to chill.
3. To make chocolate truffle, heat one-fourth cup and two tablespoons fresh cream in another small non-stick pan, but do not boil it.
4. Put the chocolate in a bowl and pour the hot cream over it. Mix well till chocolate melts completely and is well blended. Allow it to cool.

5. Place remaining one cup fresh cream in the refrigerator to chill.
6. Blend the chocolate truffle, milk powder mixture, chilled milk, chilled cream and sugar together till smooth.
7. Pour this mixture into an airtight ice cream container and let it set in a freezer. When semi set, sprinkle chocolate chips on top and let it set completely again in a freezer.
8. When ready to serve, scoop out into bowls and serve chilled.

Walnut Chocolate Fudge

INGREDIENTS

1½ cups chopped walnuts

1 tablespoon cocoa powder

Butter, for greasing

1 cup condensed milk

2 tablespoons icing sugar

½ cup grated mawa/khoya

Chocolate Truffle

½ cup chopped dark chocolate

¼ cup fresh cream

METHOD

1. To make the chocolate truffle, heat the fresh cream in a small non-stick pan. Take it off the heat and pour it over the chopped chocolate in a bowl. Mix well till the chocolate melts. Set aside to cool.

2. Grease a seven-inch by five-inch rectangular aluminium tray with butter.
3. Pour the condensed milk into another non-stick pan and cook, stirring continuously, till it is light brown in colour.
4. Add the cocoa powder, icing sugar, walnuts, mawa and chocolate truffle. Mix well and cook till the mixture begins to leave the sides of the pan.
5. Transfer this mixture into the tray and let it set at room temperature.
6. Cut into squares and serve.

Hot Chocolate Nut Sundae

INGREDIENTS

¾ cup chocolate sauce
20-25 almonds, roasted and sliced
4 scoops vanilla ice cream
4 scoops fresh strawberry ice cream
4 scoops chocolate ice cream
½ cup black grapes, halved
½ cup green grapes, halved
20-25 fresh strawberries, halved
4 oranges, separated into segments
½ cup pomegranate kernels
4 wafer biscuits, cut into triangles

METHOD

1. Select glasses for making the sundae and chill them in a refrigerator.
2. Heat the chocolate sauce in a double boiler. Just before serving, take each glass out of the refrigerator and put a quarter portion of the prepared fruit in it. On it place one scoop each of the three ice creams.
3. Immediately pour one tablespoon of hot chocolate sauce on each. Sprinkle with almonds, decorate with a wafer biscuit and serve immediately.

(Hot Chocolate Nut Sundae)

(Chocolate Pizza)

Chocolate Pizza

INGREDIENTS

¾ cup grated white chocolate + ½ cup for garnishing

1 eight-inch round sponge cake

1 cup fresh cream

2 kiwi fruit

8-10 strawberries (or 4-5 plums)

4 tinned pineapple slices

METHOD

1. Preheat oven to 190°C/375°F/Gas Mark 5.
2. Cut the sponge cake into half horizontally. Grill both the halves in the preheated oven for three minutes.
3. Heat the fresh cream in a non-stick pan. Place three-fourth cup grated white chocolate in a bowl and add the hot cream and mix till well blended and smooth.
4. Slice the kiwi fruit lengthways. Hull the strawberries and slice neatly. If you are using plums, remove the pips and slice. Slice the pineapple.

5. Remove the sponge slices from the oven and place on a plate. Spread the cream mixture equally and evenly on both the cake halves.
6. Arrange the pineapple slices attractively, followed by strawberry (or plum) slices and kiwi slices. Sprinkle the white chocolate on top.
7. Serve immediately.

Magic Chocolate Mud Pudding

INGREDIENTS

1 cup refined flour

5 tablespoons cocoa powder

60 grams butter

½ cup brown sugar

2 cups milk

½ teaspoon baking powder

½ teaspoon cinnamon powder

METHOD

1. Preheat the oven to 180°C/350°F/Gas Mark 4.
2. Lightly grease a four-inch deep glass dish or loaf tin.
3. Place the butter, half the sugar and half the milk in a pan and heat gently, stirring from time to time, until the butter has melted and all the sugar has dissolved. Remove from heat.

4. Sift the flour, baking powder, cinnamon powder and one tablespoon of cocoa powder together into the pan and stir well to mix. Pour the mixture into the greased dish or tin and level the surface.
5. Sift the remaining sugar and cocoa powder into a separate bowl and mix well. Sprinkle the mixture over the pudding mixture in the dish. Pour the remaining milk over the pudding mixture.
6. Bake for fifty minutes or until the sponge has risen to the top and is firm to the touch.
7. The pudding will separate into two layers – a gooey chocolate sauce topped with a light chocolate sponge. Serve hot.

Chocolate Burfi

INGREDIENTS

3 tablespoons cocoa powder

500 grams mawa/khoya

Oil, for greasing

½-⅓ cup powdered sugar

Edible silver foil, for decorating (optional)

METHOD

1. Crumble the mawa into fine granules. Grease a seven-inch by five-inch rectangular aluminum tray with oil and set aside.
2. Cook the mawa in a thick-bottomed non-stick pan, stirring continuously, till it melts completely and reaches a thick sauce-like consistency. Take care that it does not change colour.
3. Let it cool slightly and then add the powdered sugar and mix well.

4. Pour half of this mixture into the greased tray. Tap the tray lightly so that the mixture spreads evenly. Set aside to cool to room temperature.
5. Cook the remaining mawa mixture on low heat. Add the cocoa powder and mix well. Take it off the heat when the powder has blended well with the mawa.
6. Pour the chocolate mixture over the white mawa mixture in the tray. Again tap the tray lightly so that the mixture spreads evenly. Set aside to cool completely.
7. Cut into squares or diamonds and serve decorated with edible silver foil if desired.

Chocolate Chikki

INGREDIENTS

1 cup chopped dark chocolate

2 cups amaranth seeds

¾ cup chopped jaggery

1 tablespoon ghee

METHOD

1. Lightly roast the amaranth seeds in a deep non-stick kadai till fragrant, taking care that the colour does not change. Remove from heat. Transfer to a platter and set aside to cool.
2. Grease a clean work top with half tablespoon of ghee. In the same kadai, cook jaggery on medium-low heat till a thick syrup is formed. To test if the syrup is ready put a drop of it in a cup of cold water. If it forms a firm ball the syrup is ready.
3. Add the amaranth seeds and half tablespoon of ghee. Mix and immediately spread on the greased surface.

4. Roll out into one-inch thick sheet. Ensure that the surface is even. Let it cool slightly. Cut neatly into one-and-half-inch squares.
5. Place the dark chocolate in a microwave-safe bowl and melt in a microwave oven on HIGH for thirty seconds.
6. Take the pan off the heat and allow the chocolate to cool, stirring continuously, to 30°C.
7. Dip a piece of amaranth seeds chikki half way into the melted chocolate. Place it on a silicon sheet till chocolate sets. Serve immediately.

(Chocolate Chikki)

(Chocolate Kalakand)

Chocolate Kalakand

INGREDIENTS

2 tablespoons cocoa powder

2 litres (10 cups) milk

⅛ teaspoon crushed alum

¾ cup sugar

2 tablespoons ghee + for greasing

2 tablespoons liquid glucose

Chocolate shavings, as required

METHOD

1. Grease a seven-inch by five-inch rectangular aluminium tray with ghee.
2. Boil the milk in a large non-stick pan on high heat. Add the alum and sugar and continue to cook, stirring continuously, for about an hour or till the milk becomes grainy and thick.
3. Add the ghee and glucose. Mix well and continue to cook till the mixture begins to coat the back of a ladle. Add the cocoa powder and mix well.
4. Transfer the mixture into the greased tray and set aside to cool to room temperature and set. Cut into squares; decorate with chocolate shavings and serve.

Chocolate Modak

INGREDIENTS

¾ cup Basmati rice flour

A pinch of salt

1 teaspoon oil + for greasing

Pure ghee, for serving

Stuffing

½ cup chopped dark chocolate

1½ cups grated fresh coconut

1 cup grated jaggery

1 tablespoon roasted poppy seeds

A pinch of green cardamom powder

A pinch of nutmeg powder

METHOD

1. Heat three-fourth cup of water with salt and one teaspoon oil in a deep non-stick pan.
2. When it comes to a boil, reduce heat and add the rice flour in a steady flow, stirring continuously to prevent lumps from forming. Cover the pan with a deep lid and pour some water into the lid. Cook on low heat for three minutes.

3. Remove the lid, sprinkle some cold water on the rice flour and cover again with the lid with water in it and cook for further three minutes. Repeat this process twice more. Take the pan off the heat and keep it covered for two minutes.
4. Transfer the mixture onto a large plate (parat), grease your palms with oil and knead the dough till smooth and pliable. The dough should not stick to your palms. Rest the dough covered with a damp cloth.
5. To make the stuffing, combine the coconut and jaggery in a non-stick pan and cook on medium heat till most of the moisture dries up.
6. Make sure that you do not overcook the mixture. Add the roasted poppy seeds, cardamom powder and nutmeg powder and mix well. Take the pan off the heat and add chocolate and mix well. Set aside to cool.
7. Divide the coconut mixture into eight equal portions. Divide the dough into eight equal portions and shape them into balls.
8. Grease your fingers and shape each ball into a deep bowl of three-inch diameter. Press the edges to reduce the thickness.
9. Place a portion of the stuffing in the centre, pleat the edges of the dough neatly, sealing them well as you go along. Pinch the top to form a tip.

10. Heat sufficient water in a steamer. Place the modak on a perforated plate, place the plate in the steamer, cover the steamer and steam for ten to twelve minutes.

11. Serve hot modak drizzled with pure ghee.

Chocolate Peda

INGREDIENTS

½ cup grated dark chocolate

2 cups mawa/khoya, crumbled

¼ cup sugar

¼ teaspoon liquid glucose

8 cashew nuts, halved horizontally

METHOD

1. Heat a non-stick pan; add the mawa and sauté on low heat, stirring continuously, for fifteen minutes. Transfer into a bowl.
2. Cook the sugar with one-fourth cup water in another non-stick pan on low heat for thirty minutes to make a syrup of one-string consistency. Add the liquid glucose and stir till it blends well.

3. Once the mawa cools slightly, add the syrup and mix well.
4. Melt the chocolate in the microwave on HIGH and whisk till smooth. Add this to the mawa mixture and mix well.
5. When the mixture cools, divide into twelve equal portions and shape into balls. Press lightly and arrange in small paper cups.
6. Decorate with cashew nuts and serve.

Chocolate and Nut Karanji

INGREDIENTS

1½ cups refined flour

3 tablespoons pure ghee

Oil for deep-frying

Stuffing

½ cup grated dark chocolate

¼ cup chopped almonds

¼ cup chopped walnuts

½ cup grated mawa/khoya

2 tablespoons powdered sugar

METHOD

1. Put the flour in a deep bowl. Add the ghee and two to three tablespoons of chilled water or chilled milk.
2. Knead into a medium-soft dough, adding more chilled water or milk as you go along. Divide into small balls and let them rest, covered with a damp cloth.

3. To make the stuffing, mix the mawa, powdered sugar, walnuts, almonds and grated chocolate in a bowl. Chill it in the refrigerator for about ten minutes.
4. Roll out the dough balls into small round puri. Place a puri on the worktop; moisten its edges.
5. Place some stuffing in the centre and fold one side of the puri over the other. Press the edges to seal and further twist the edges with your finger tips in a decorative manner. Or cut the edges with a serrated cutter. You can also make the karanji using a mould.
6. Keep the karanji in the refrigerator for thirty to forty minutes.
7. Heat sufficient oil in a kadai. Deep-fry the karanjis, a few at a time, till light brown. Drain on absorbent paper.
8. Serve hot or allow them to cool to room temperature and store in an airtight container.

(Chocolate and Nut Karanji)

Chocolate Sticks
Chocolate Leaves
Chocolate Flowers
Chocolate Curls
Chocolate Arcs
Chocolate Hearts

Chocolate Leaves

INGREDIENTS

1 cup chopped dark chocolate

A few leaves of mint or carom

METHOD

1. Melt the chocolate in a microwave-safe bowl in the microwave on HIGH for one minute. Remove the bowl from the microwave and whisk well, till the temperature comes down to 30°C.
2. With the help of a brush, apply the melted chocolate on the front side of the leaves and place them on the tray. Refrigerate till the chocolate sets.
3. Remove from refrigerator and carefully peel off the leaves.
4. Store the chocolate leaves in an airtight container and place in a refrigerator till further use.

Chocolate Hearts

INGREDIENTS

1 cup chopped dark chocolate

METHOD

1. Place an OHP sheet (see note in Chocolate Arcs) on a working surface.
2. Melt the chocolate in a microwave-safe bowl in the microwave on HIGH for one minute. Remove the bowl from the microwave and whisk till the chocolate cools down to 30°C.
3. Pour the melted chocolate into a piping bag, cut the tip to make a very small hole to allow the melted chocolate to pour out easily.
4. Make outlines of heart shapes with the piping bag on the OHP sheets and fill them up with chocolate lines, keeping a small loop empty.
5. Place the sheets in the refrigerator and allow the hearts to set till completely firm.
6. Peel off the hearts gently from the sheets and store them till further use.

Chocolate Flowers

INGREDIENTS

1 cup chopped dark chocolate

METHOD

1. Melt the chocolate in a microwave-safe bowl in the microwave on HIGH for one minute. Remove the bowl from the microwave and whisk till the chocolate cools down to 30°C.
2. Pour the chocolate on a silicon sheet and spread evenly with the help of a palate knife.
3. When the chocolate is half set, using a flower shaped cutter, make demarcations on the chocolate. Refrigerate for ten to fifteen minutes.
4. Gently remove the flowers with the help of palate knife and use as required.

Chocolate Sticks

INGREDIENTS

1 cup chopped dark chocolate

METHOD

1. Melt the chocolate in a microwave-safe bowl in the microwave on HIGH for one minute. Remove the bowl from the microwave and whisk briskly till the chocolate cools down to 30°C. Pour the chocolate on a silicon sheet and spread evenly with the help of a palate knife.

3. When the chocolate is half set, with the help of a scale and knife, make demarcations of desired width on the chocolate to make the sticks. Refrigerate for ten to fifteen minutes. Peel off the sticks with the help of palate knife and use as required.

Chocolate Curls

INGREDIENTS

1 slab (approx 500 grams) dark chocolate, at room temperature

METHOD

1. Place the chocolate slab on a worktop. With the help of a ring cutter, scrape the chocolate so that the chocolate scrapes in curls. Cover a tray with cling film and place the prepared chocolate curls on it. Chocolate curls can be used to decorate Eggless Black Forest Gateau.

{Note: The narrower side of the chocolate bar helps to create small curls, while the broader side is best to create larger curls.}

Chocolate Arcs

INGREDIENTS

1 cup chopped dark chocolate

METHOD

1. Melt the chocolate in a double boiler. Remove from heat and stir well to temper the chocolate till the temperature falls to 30°C.

2. Cut an OHP sheet (see note) into an eight by one-and-a-half-inch piece and place it on a worktop.
3. Pour half the melted chocolate on the OHP sheet and with the help of the spatula spread the chocolate evenly. Continue spreading till it just starts setting. Do not overwork, or else it will have a grainy texture.
4. Remove the excess chocolate from the sides and put it in the chocolate bowl. When the chocolate is still semi-hard hold the OHP sheet in your hand and give it a turn so that both the ends rest on the plate and form an arc shape.
5. Refrigerate for ten minutes. Remove and peel off the OHP sheet carefully. Repeat the procedure for the remaining chocolate.
6. Place the chocolate arcs in an airtight container and place in a refrigerator till further use.

Note: OHP (over head projector) sheets are thin plastic sheets. Flexible and easy to cut with scissors, they are excellent for making decorative shapes with melted chocolate. Also known as transparencies, they are readily available in stationery shops.

Measurements

Ingredients	Quantity/No	Weight	Ingredients	Quantity/No	Weight
Almonds	10	15 grams	Cheese spread	1 cup	180 grams
Alum, crushed	1 teaspoon	8 grams	Chocolate sauce	1 tablespoon	15 grams
Apple	1 medium	120 grams	Chocolate truffle	1 tablespoon	12 grams
Baking powder	1 teaspoon	3 grams	Cocoa powder	1 cup	120 grams
Black grapes	10	40 grams	Coffee powder	1 teaspoon	5 grams
Brown sugar	1 cup	200 grams	Condensed milk	1 cup	400 grams
Butter	1 tablespoon	15 grams	Dark chocolate, grated	1 cup	100 grams
Butter	1 cup	150 grams	Dark chocolate, melted	1 cup	300 grams
Butter, melted	1 cup	200 grams	Fresh cream	1 cup	200 mls
Butterscotch pearls, crushed	1 tablespoon	10 grams	Fresh cream	1 tablespoon	15 mls
Caramel fudge	1 cup	350 grams	Fresh yeast	1 tablespoon	10 grams
Cashew nut paste	1 tablespoon	15 grams	Gelatine	1 tablespoon	15 grams
Castor sugar	1 cup	125 grams			

Ingredients	Quantity/No	Weight
Ghee	1 tablespoon	15 grams
Honey	1 tablespoon	15 mls
Icecream	1 cup	150 grams
Icing sugar	1 cup	125 grams
Jaggery, grated	1 cup	200 grams
Lemon juice	1 teaspoon	5 mls
Liquid glucose	1 tablespoon	15 grams
Mawa (khoya)	1 cup	180 grams
Milk	1 cup	200 mls
Milk chocolate, chopped	1 cup	125 grams
Muesli	1 cup	100 grams
Nutella	1 tablespoon	18 grams
Nutmeg powder	1 teaspoon	4 grams
Oats	1 cup	170 grams

Ingredients	Quantity/No	Weight
Peanut butter	1 tablespoon	20 grams
Pears	1 medium	150 grams
Poppy seeds	1 tablespoon	12.5 grams
Powdered sugar	1 tablespoon	15 grams
Rajgira grains	1 cup	210 grams
Ripe mango pulp	1 cup	280 grams
Rum	1 tablespoon	15 mls
Salt	1 teaspoon	5 grams
Star anise	1	2 grams
Sugar	1 cup	250 grams
Tinned cherries, without syrup	1 cup	210 grams
Vanilla essence	1 teaspoon	5 mls
Walnuts	1 cup	120 grams
Whipped cream	1 cup	150 grams